Praise for
EWOC and *Unite & Win*

"EWOC has produced a magnificent, concise, and readable text directed to and for workers who want to organize against injustice. The booklet uses clear examples and has specific suggestions on what can be done to fight the power of the employer class."

—Bill Fletcher, Jr., trade unionist and writer

"People often contact me asking how they can unionize. I always point them towards EWOC. This publication shows why. In easy-to-understand language, it tells you everything you need to know about the union organizing process, taking you from 'mildly curious' to 'marching on the boss' in less than fifty pages. A lot of people never get around to organizing simply because they don't know how. This guide is all you need to illuminate the path."

—Hamilton Nolan, *The Hammer: Power, Inequality, and the Struggle for the Soul of Labor*

"*Unite and Win* is a godsend. Organizing a union is intimidating for many workers, the majority of whom have never been in a union, much less formed one themselves. This guide from EWOC demystifies the process, addressing many of the questions, both big and small, that workers will encounter along the path to unionizing. EWOC has done heroic work these past few years, filling a gap in the existing labor movement by supporting unorganized workers of all kinds as they take their first collective actions; their use of that experience as a basis for this organizing guide is a gift to us all. Finally — a comprehensive, accessible resource that I can send people who ask me how, exactly, to unionize their workplace."

—Alex Press, Labor Journalist at *Jacobin* Magazine

"EWOC's new handbook for organizers is a critical resource for the new labor movement. And it could not come at a better time. In a moment when workers most need a groundswell of rank-and-file leadership to fight for democratic workplaces, this guide provides a clear how-to. In four concise lessons, workplace organizers will learn to build power with their coworkers and take action to win improvements on the job."

—Daisy Pitkin, *On the Line: A Story of Class, Solidarity, and Two Women's Epic Fight to Build a Union*

"Talking to your co-workers is the first step to gaining power on the job. When the pandemic hit, EWOC started helping workers build unity and power on the job, from bus drivers to baristas. This book is for anyone thinking, 'We need a union around here!' It helps you get started and figure out what to do next."

—Luis Feliz Leon, Staff Writer and Organizer with Labor Notes

"Indispensable reading for anybody thinking about organizing their workplace. A lively and accessible step-by-step guide to unionizing, Unite and Win can help turn today's labor uptick into a national working-class upsurge. Get a copy for yourself — and a handful for your co-workers."

—Eric Blanc, *Red State Revolt: The Teachers' Strike Wave and Working-Class Politics*

"EWOC is a bold and innovative labor project that has racked up an incredible number of organizing wins among workers of all kinds throughout the country. The lessons they have learned along the way that are collected here add up to more than just a guide or a manual. This is a blueprint for how to transform your life and those of your coworkers, to reshape conditions at the place where workers spend the majority of our lives: the workplace."

—Micah Uetricht, Editor of *Jacobin* Magazine, *Strike for America: Chicago Teachers Against Austerity*

Emergency Workplace
Organizing Committee
(EWOC)

Unite & Win

The Workplace
Organizer's Handbook

EDITED BY
Daphna Thier

DESIGN BY
Stephen Crowe

ILLUSTRATIONS BY
Down the Street Designs

HaymarketBooks
Chicago, Illinois

Published in 2024 by
Haymarket Books
P.O. Box 180165
Chicago, IL 60618
www.haymarketbooks.org

ISBN: 9798888902691

Distributed to the trade in the US through Consortium Book Sales
and Distribution (www.cbsd.com) and internationally through Ingram
Publisher Services International (www.ingramcontent.com).

Special discounts are available for bulk purchases by organizations
and institutions. Please email info@haymarketbooks.org for more
information.

Layout and design by Stephen Crowe.

Printed in Canada by union labor.

Library of Congress Cataloging-in-Publication data is available.

10 9 8 7 6 5 4 3 2 1

Table of Contents

What's in this handbook?

The Emergency Workplace Organizing Committee (EWOC) has trained and supported thousands of workers just like you. We've trained non-profit workers, school bus drivers, and early childhood educators on how to talk to their coworkers about collective action. We've supported workers in retail stores and graduate programs when they marched on their bosses. We've coached pizzeria workers, baristas, and rock climbing gym workers when they decided to unionize. We wrote this guide to share the knowledge we gathered in all of those experiences to empower you and your coworkers to win the workplace improvements you deserve.

This guide serves as a companion to the EWOC Foundational Training Program. You will find a series of lessons here that correspond with the program's four training sessions. Each lesson covers a different core element of organizing at the workplace – the organizing committee, the organizing conversation, collective action, and inoculation against the boss's response.

There are many forms that your efforts to win positive changes at work can take. You may decide to focus on specific changes to your workplace that a majority of your coworkers want to see in an issue-based campaign, or you may pursue unionization. Even within union drives, there are different models – you may affiliate with an established union, or you may choose to file for an independent union. You may even decide to act as a union before you have support from a majority of coworkers, something called "pre-majority unionism."

Whatever your path is, at its core, it involves organizing. And that's what this handbook is all about.

You can use this guide to review the lessons at the end of each corresponding Foundational Training session.

If you are not currently enrolled in one of our trainings, each lesson has a recommended accompanying video for you to view before or after your reading. You can find those online at workerorganizing.org.

But… organizing is a team project! And the materials in here are intended as supplements to group discussions. So find yourself a buddy or a group of coworkers, and follow along with our videos and materials to talk about your organizing plans.

Organizing Your Coworkers for Change

What Is Organizing?

Over decades of struggle, our movement has learned crucial methods for building worker power in the workplace. Workplace organizing usually requires steps such as the following:

→ Reaching out to diverse groups of workers, finding common interests, overcoming differences, and building relationships

→ Asking coworkers to join an organizing committee

→ Planning and carrying out actions to improve working conditions

→ Recruiting others to help plan and execute tasks, come to meetings, or participate in actions

→ Helping others develop confidence in themselves and their coworkers

→ Having one-on-one conversations with coworkers about forming a union

→ Preparing your coworkers for what the bosses will try to do to stop the union

In organizing your workplace, you must reach out to every single coworker. And you need to find a way to connect with people whom you may not find it so easy to connect with. This will be difficult but it's worth it, because to win any demands or a union at your workplace, you need to have support from a strong majority.

This guide will give you the tools you need to organize your coworkers so you can win dignity and respect, better working conditions, real job security, and a real democratic say at work. By learning to organize you can be part of rebuilding a fighting labor movement with the power to take on the billionaire class and transform society.

Why We Organize

Organizing is how we change the world. We organize collectively because there is power and safety in numbers.

When a workplace is organized, it means the workers have come together and built a structure to fight for justice at work. We can win dignity and respect, better salaries and benefits, and protections from abusive bosses. Workers who are organized have far more power together than an individual on their own.

Without our labor, there is no company, no institution, no product, no service.

Organizing in the workplace is especially effective because as workers, we provide the labor. Without our labor, there is no company, no institution, no product, no service. That gives us leverage and power when we act together.

So why isn't every workplace organized? In addition to there being historically weak labor laws in the US that can make unions difficult to form, our bosses — and their bosses, all the way up to the CEO and the shareholders — profit more when we aren't organized. If workers aren't organized, then our bosses can pay us less and keep more revenue for themselves; they can treat us poorly and fire us for no good reason; they can make every decision by themselves to benefit only themselves. That's why bosses will do anything they can to prevent workers from organizing: they want the workplace to stay in their control, forcing us to choose between obeying and quitting.

But even though it takes time and effort, any worker, anywhere, can organize and win.

📖 In this guide, we are primarily focused on **new organizing,** which refers to organizing workers at a workplace that does not currently have a union, often with the intent to unionize and win a first contract.

What Is a Union?

A union is an organization of coworkers who join together to improve their working conditions. If the union has proven that it represents a majority of workers, the employer is required by law to "recognize" the union and begin to bargain in good faith.

One benefit of a recognized union is that it puts into legally binding contracts your terms of employment, and enables you and your coworkers to negotiate those terms. A contract makes it illegal for the employer to unilaterally roll back your gains.

Across the board, workers in unionized jobs have:

→ Higher pay: Union workers earn 17% more than non-union workers.

→ Better health insurance: More than 90% of unionized workers have access to employer-provided health insurance, compared with 68% of non-union workers.

→ Better retirement benefits: 93% of unionized workers in private industry have access to employer-sponsored retirement plans, compared with 66% of non-union workers.

→ A stronger voice on the job: Unions negotiate schedules; health, safety, and anti-harassment policies; promotional opportunities; and job security.

Unions can also be our voice in the broader community. There is a long history of organized workers winning major social gains like the eight-hour workday, the weekend, social security, civil rights, immigrant rights, and more. At their best, unions don't advocate just for their members; they fight for the entire working class, including those workers who aren't and never will be union members.

Union Members Are the Union

The union isn't an organization outside of the members. It may affiliate with a national "parent union," often called an "international," which provides it with helpful resources, including legal counsel to navigate labor laws. But members are the ultimate decision-makers and the ones who elect their leadership.

The union isn't an organization outside of the members.

In the best examples, union members are involved in every step of the contract negotiation process. Workers in a union can set their own bargaining agenda and vote on contracts. They often vote to take collective action if the boss refuses to meet their terms during negotiations. Democracy in a union allows workers of all races, ethnicities, genders, and sexual orientations to have a voice.

Independent unions

In some cases where workers have not found a suitable established union, they will decide to form their own independent union. This union will have no formal ties to a national or international union. It also often means that its members are filing for a union election themselves.

For some workplaces there can be benefits to this approach. But filing independently is a tricky and bureaucratic process, so don't do it alone! EWOC has resources and organizers who can walk you through the process so that you don't miss deadlines or make other small mistakes that can disqualify your filing.

> ▌ Union members are often referred to as the **"rank and file."** Rank-and-file activity and leadership is the central element in the strategy laid out in this guide.

Pre-majority Unionism

In some cases, such as with public-sector workers in many states, workers can't get legal union recognition and a contract (see Limits of the NLRA sidebar on page 16 for more information on this). Or maybe they believe that winning an election will take many years, as is sometimes the case for workers in very large workplaces.

In these situations, there's another kind of unionism outside the traditional path for organizing: pre-majority unions.

In its broadest sense, pre-majority unionism is a union model in which workers organize and act like a union, sometimes even collecting dues — even though they have not filed for NLRB recognition. This can be a viable alternative for those seeking to win gains at work.

You can find much more information about pre-majority unionism on our website, workerorganizing.org. If you reach out to EWOC for support, experienced EWOC organizers can help you navigate the processes of pre-majority unionism.

NON-UNION

Gary has to go to HR alone to complain about harassment.

UNION

Gail files a grievance with the entire union backing her.

NON-UNION

Gary has to negotiate a new salary one-on-one with the boss.

UNION

Gail has a whole bargaining committee to negotiate.

NON-UNION

Gary feels underqualified for a new responsibility at work and doesn't know what to do.

UNION

Gail turns to her union steward for guidance and help in finding skills training.

NON-UNION

After a workplace injury, Gary has to figure out how to file worker's compensation by himself.

UNION

Gail asks for help from the union steward and others who've done it before.

NON-UNION

Gary gets written up and then fired with almost no opportunity for him to question his treatment.

UNION

Gail's boss has to give her notice before he writes her up, and then a union steward is in the room during the discipline meeting to defend her.

📖 A **union steward,** also called a shop steward, is a coworker and member of the union whom coworkers elect to represent them and the union to management.

What is the NLRA?

The right to unionize is protected by the National Labor Relations Act (NLRA, also known as the Wagner Act). The National Labor Relations Board (NLRB) is the federal agency that enforces the NLRA.

Before the NLRA was passed in 1935, unions were often considered criminal conspiracies. But with the law's passage, workers won the right to bargain collectively and strike. It also codified what it meant for employers to engage in Unfair Labor Practices and required them to bargain in good faith. The NLRA protects private-sector workers and cannot be overridden by local laws. Bosses have spent decades lobbying to erode it.

The Limits of the NLRA

Public-sector employees are not covered by the National Labor Relations Act. Laws governing public-sector collective bargaining vary greatly by state. In some states, laws apply statewide as well as at the municipal level. In others, no statewide collective bargaining law exists, but some local jurisdictions might have laws covering their employees. Some states don't require collective bargaining, but they also don't prohibit it. The Carolinas, Tennessee, Georgia, and Texas currently outright prohibit public-sector workers from collective bargaining. However, in accordance with their First Amendment rights, workers in those states can still form non-recognized unions (see explanation of "Pre-majority Unionism" on page 13 in the introduction).

Other worksites that don't fall under the jurisdiction of the NLRB are federal sector workplaces, where the Federal Labor Relations Authority governs labor relations. Likewise, the railway and airline industries are covered by the Railway Labor Act.

The NLRA also excludes from protection agricultural and farm workers, domestic workers, gig workers, and independent contractors. However, some of these workers may have specific organizing protections through state laws.

If you are angry about your working conditions but fall within an unprotected category as a worker, don't despair. Even in situations with no formal collective bargaining, workers have formed and joined non-recognized unions or associations to advocate for their interests in the workplace and in the state legislature. They've taken collective action, and even gone on to strike. When workers come together, they can win gains even in legally unfavorable terrain.

How Can Workers Form A Legally Recognized Union?

Federal law provides two ways that private-sector workers can form a union legally recognized by employers: **recognition by election** and **recognition by card check**.

Recognition by election

Recognition by election is the most common way workers form a union. This is a campaign coordinated by workers to gain recognition from their employer for collective bargaining purposes. The campaign involves:

→ Workers organizing and gathering signatures from a majority of employees in the proposed bargaining unit — the group of workers to be represented by the union — on union authorization cards or via a petition. Deciding whether to have coworkers sign union cards or add their names to a petition demanding recognition is a tactical choice you will have to make. If you want to build support, sometimes creating a petition signed by many coworkers makes more of an impact on hesitant coworkers.

→ Filing a petition with the NLRB to hold a secret-ballot election. Legally, only 30% of employees must petition for an election, but most union campaigns will not file for an election unless they have signatures from a majority of the workers.

→ If a majority of voting workers vote for the union, the employer must recognize the union for purposes of collective bargaining. If the workers do not secure a majority vote, then the union is not formally recognized and the employer is not required to bargain with the workers. A tied election is a lost election.

Defining the Bargaining Unit in an Election

One tactic employers use to delay or undermine elections and negotiations is to contest the size and scope of the bargaining unit. For example, the boss might argue that the unit is actually larger than its members claim it is, and that they do not in fact represent enough of the

> **Bargaining units** are groups of workers who share clear "community interests" and constitute a distinct, recognizable, and homogeneous group of workers to be represented by a particular union. Bargaining unit members must be easily identifiable based on their job classification, department, location, skill, or other factor.

unit to qualify for an election. The boss often does this because they know a significant component of this 'expanded' bargaining unit is less organized or even anti-union. Or, the boss might argue that the union can only represent a smaller segment of the workforce. Again, they will often zero in on less-organized departments or categories of workers.

Who's legally excluded from the bargaining unit?

→ A "confidential employee," a term referring to someone who has duties involving access to information on the boss's labor relations or bargaining strategy.

→ A manager who has the authority to hire and fire, offer promotions and bonuses, transfer or schedule other employees, and influence the company's policies. (A supervisor though they may perform managerial duties, can still be included in the unit if they don't have the authority to hire and fire, offer promotions and bonuses, transfer or schedule other workers.)

→ Any workers who do not meet the criteria or classification that define the bargaining unit.

Recognition by card check

Recognition by card check, or voluntary recognition, is the other, much rarer way for workers to form a union. Here, a majority of workers in a proposed bargaining unit sign cards indicating that they want to be represented by a union, and the employer agrees voluntarily to recognize the union as the legal representative of the workers, thus averting the need for a secret-ballot election.

A card-check campaign is much fairer than an election campaign, because the employer is not waging an anti-union campaign to undermine the will of the majority of the workers.

Although federal law clearly gives private-sector workers the right to organize a union without fear of employer interference, in reality, most employers vigorously oppose their employees' efforts to form a union by running aggressive (and often illegal) anti-union campaigns aimed at scaring and intimidating the workers from supporting the union.

So, while the steps to winning a union are straightforward, workers still have to run smart and strategic campaigns to stay ahead of aggressive opposition from their employers.

📖 A **local union** is an affiliate of a statewide, national, or international union and represents one or more bargaining units. Also called "local association," or "local" for short, it has its own set of bylaws and elected leadership.

What Is in a Contract?

A union contract, also known as a Collective Bargaining Agreement (CBA), is a legally binding document that spells out the terms and conditions of employment for unionized workers. It is negotiated between the union representing the workers and the employer, and typically covers issues such as wages, benefits, staffing, working hours, job security, and workplace safety.

Union contracts ensure that workers have a real voice in their workplace and are treated fairly and with respect. Before a contract goes into effect, it must be voted on by the workers.

The Basics of Union Elections

After workers submit cards asking for an election, and the minimum number of signatures have been confirmed, the NLRB sets the election date. Though there are rules the NLRB sets to ensure elections are conducted in an expeditious manner, often the employer will attempt to slow down this process in order to have more time to run an anti-union campaign. The organizing committee should anticipate this strategy and have a plan for how to counter it and keep the momentum on their side.

Once the NLRB sets the election date, the leadership team or organizing committee (OC, more on this term in the next section) should make sure they know where every pro-union worker will be on that day and get their commitment to vote. For workers who are not going to be at work that day, the committee needs a plan for how to get them to vote, because on election day, its job is to get every "yes" voter to the polling place.

Alternatively, some elections are done by mail-in ballots. In that case, the agency running the election (the NLRB or state labor board, for example) mails the ballots. These need to be marked and returned by a certain date to be valid.

When the election is over and the NLRB is counting the votes, the job of the OC is to monitor and ensure that all eligible votes are counted.

Election victories are always exhilarating, emotional moments for workers. Your OC should definitely take time to celebrate and bask in the incredible achievements that you have made. But once the union wins the election, the work is not done. The OC needs to begin preparing for the contract campaign and contract negotiations.

This is because, in practice, even once an election has been won, employers often still do everything to avoid bargaining in good faith with the new union. Winning a good contract can often be an even greater challenge than a union election.

Lesson One

The Organizing Committee Model

How to build and run your team

The organizing committee (OC) is a group of coworkers leading a workplace campaign.

It is responsible for developing and implementing a plan, which includes:

→ Creating a list of all the workers, mapping their relationships with each other, and identifying potential leaders

→ Building support for the union among their coworkers and educating them about the union

→ Building up new leaders who can help the OC grow

→ Helping coworkers overcome fear and preparing them for the employer's anti-union campaign (more on this in Lesson 4: Inoculation and the Boss Campaign)

→ Collecting signatures on authorization cards

→ Working with other recognized unions and community allies

Why Must You Build an Organizing Committee?

An effective OC that truly represents the workforce is essential to winning a union recognition campaign.

One person or a small group or clique of workers cannot build and sustain the strong cohesion necessary for effectively standing up to a boss's anti-union campaign.

The OC provides leadership for the union campaign. It should aim to represent at least 10% of the workforce, and should have a representative makeup that covers demographics, worker cliques, and languages, along with all departments, shifts, and worksite locations. The committee needs to communicate effectively and regularly with all coworkers so it can help them see through divisions, overcome fear, and move into action.

A good OC knows its coworkers well and can identify the most widely felt issues in the workplace as well as any vulnerabilities and fears. OC members must both be sensitive to people who may be more vulnerable to retaliation or job loss because of discrimination based on race, ethnicity, gender, or immigration status, and supportive of those workers when they are ready to take action. The OC acts in ways that build trust.

” Trevor, rock climbing gym worker:

"When we started I was still kind of junior, I'd been hired only a few months before… but one of our most senior workers at the gym joined the OC and was someone that people looked to and trusted. Not someone who was just mouthing off and complaining, but who had something to back up what they were saying."

The most effective organizing committees include workers who are real leaders from all parts of the workforce and have the trust of their coworkers.

Building an Organizing Committee and Developing Leadership

Your OC needs to map out existing networks in your workplace, beginning by thinking about your own relationships and who you know as real leaders and trusted coworkers. If you don't personally know those leaders, you need to figure out how to meet them.

Ask yourself, who at your workplace would you turn to if you had a question, had a problem with a manager, or needed help finding resources? Who at your workplace organizes the group hangouts, the birthday cards, the carpools? Who at your workplace do people gravitate to? Who do people listen to? If that's not you yet, that's okay! But you do want to find a way to recruit some of those people who are already leaders.

Some tasks for your coworkers might include:

→ Getting an employee list for their department
→ Helping to set up a meeting with one of their coworkers
→ Identifying who they think are potential leaders
→ Finding out what improvements their coworkers would like to see
→ Getting signatures on a petition or authorization cards
→ Participating in a workplace action

Your OC will then have one-on-one conversations with coworkers, building trust and learning what improvements they'd like to see in the workplace. Often this involves asking if they might be interested in forming a union, though depending on your strategy that might not be the priority for the first conversation. These conversations need to be carried out thoughtfully to make sure that the boss does not find out. Often, meeting coworkers individually or in small groups outside of work is the best and safest way to have conversations and build relationships. Phone calls are more effective (and safer) than texts.

Throughout every stage of the campaign, the OC must continue to identify and recruit established leaders in the workplace, while also developing potential leaders' skills and knowledge. As potential OC members are identified, they should be given small tasks that gradually increase in difficulty and risk.

As people take on more tasks and show their reliability, they should be invited onto the OC and given more leadership responsibilities, including helping to identify and recruit more coworkers as organizers. The OC members need to hold each other accountable for carrying out the tasks that they have taken responsibility for.

Developing leadership and organizing skills is an ongoing process even after winning the election and establishing the union. A strong democratic union depends on having strong leadership throughout the workplace.

Charting Your Workplace

In order to do all of these things, you and your OC must track your conversations and record notes in an organized chart of all of your coworkers.

This chart should include a row for every worker and columns detailing:

→ Name, job, shift, and personal contact info
→ Major concerns a worker has (at work and at home)
→ Friendships and cliques
→ Assessment
→ Tasks completed and actions taken

The chart will help you ensure you have the support you need throughout your workplace, and strong relationships with a majority of your coworkers. You'll be able to track things such as which issues are universal; who knows who in your workplace and what departments they work in; where are your weak spots; who's friends with the boss; and even how many people have participated in a particular action. Combined, these pieces of information tell you whether your campaign is in fact building support, thereby taking most of the guesswork out of the process. It will also ensure you don't miss a single coworker, even in a larger workplace.

The list-building, one-on-one conversations with coworkers, and identification of leaders and workplace issues are instrumental in build-

📖 **Assessment** usually refers to how you think the person you're speaking with feels about unionization: Do they support it? Are they against it? Undecided? Unless you feel certain that this coworker will jeopardize the campaign if you are too honest with them, avoid jumping to conclusions before making your ask and seeing how they respond.

ing a communication network in the workplace, and should be done throughout the campaign.

Remember, your boss also has a chart like this for their anti-union campaign! Not having a chart of your own will leave you vulnerable to their counter-campaign.

Finally, your chart is a confidential document. We recommend you not share it with anyone outside your trusted circle of OC members. You can share some — but not all — of this information with potential leaders you are building up. And don't ever share your chart over work emails.

▪ Socialize before you organize!

It's important to find ways to gather coworkers for social activities and enjoy food and drinks together early on in the process (and throughout it). Strong personal relationships build trust and solidarity. And a fun community is one that is easy to keep people invested in it.

❞ Clarissa, supermarket worker:

"People want to let loose after a long shift. So it's not as difficult as you would think to get a group of people out. Since turnover is high, we even used people's last day as an excuse to gather."

The Organizing Conversation

The organizing conversation is the basic building block of organizing. Getting to know your coworkers is critical to any organizing effort. The organizing conversation, a conversation that can move people to take action and organize, consists of these basic and time-tested steps:

1	Introduction	Who are you? What are your concerns?
2	Get the issues	What does your coworker care about?
3	Agitation	Why that's unfair. And, you're not alone!
4	Plan to Win	Why collective action? What's the plan?
5	Inoculation	Prepare for your boss's response.
6	Call the Question	Ask them to take action.

In-person and one-on-one conversations strengthen relationships and foster trust. They also allow for more back-and-forth, which is important in situations where people have a lot of questions, concerns, or ideas to share.

❞ Kelly, cleaning supplies company worker:

"The two biggest obstacles I faced in my campaign are, one, the fact that we all saw each other only in the mornings, and then everyone dispersed and I was the only one left in the office. And two, the high turnover rate. In tackling those two things, I had to be bold. I had to introduce myself to new employees, I had to introduce myself to my coworkers who I had just met the day before and say, 'Hey, do you mind if I get your cell phone number?'"

Not all of the above steps happen in every conversation — this is just a general guide. But it can be helpful to look at this model before having a conversation. If you remember one or two points from it, then it was helpful.

You might also look over this table after a conversation with a buddy or your OC, and ask yourself what you might have said differently. This will prepare you for future conversations and help you to not feel down on yourself if a conversation didn't go the way you imagined it would. The most important thing is to be yourself, be natural, and follow the flow of conversation.

It's a good rule of thumb to listen as much as or more than you talk.

Our coworkers' issues are the primary motivation for them to get involved in organizing, so it's important to learn about them as people and about their issues.

" Clarissa, supermarket worker:

"Issues of favoritism and unfairness are common at my workplace. So I like to ask, 'Do you have a favorite supervisor?' and 'Do you have a supervisor that you don't get along with?' That really leads the conversation to why they have issues.

"I've also had success talking about interactions with customers, or sections and shifts that people like working best. Or talking about how people are coming and going, why they think that is, how they feel about it. I also like to get to know their personal life, whether they have family, if they're a student, if they have another job. Things that they deal with outside of work that affect them at work.

"I've found those to be successful segues into, 'What do you think would be a fair wage?' 'What do you think about the benefits we're getting?' Or, 'Did you hear they're slashing their contribution to retirement plans?'"

If you want to learn about your coworkers' issues, it's a good rule of thumb to listen as much as or more than you talk. Workers won't find this conversation important unless they feel personally fired up about the issues you're talking about. Then show them how their issues

connect with the organizing. In the case of an organizing campaign for a union, connect their issues with the organizing and bargaining that workers will be doing through that union.

🎤 Keith, remote software engineer:

"You've got to talk to everyone, and you've got to talk to everyone multiple times. I found some people that I didn't need to talk to every week; some people are in it and they're not going to change. But some people are a little more on the fence. Those are the conversations that I would come back to and check in regularly."

When you agitate coworkers, you validate the unfairness of their concerns and show them their coworkers feel the same way.

Once you've agitated coworkers, you can provide them with concrete hope by telling them about the OC's plans. Your coworkers won't want to take action unless they genuinely believe there's a way to tackle those issues, a plan to win.

For example, in a union drive, you educate your coworkers about what unions are and how they function. You talk to them about the power and safety in numbers, and the need for a majority of workers to stand together and represent yourselves. You can strengthen your case by sharing examples of how other workers have won through similar methods.

Through one-on-ones, you also prepare your coworkers for how the boss will respond in order to stop the organizing. This process is often called "inoculation." (See Lesson 4: Inoculation and the Boss Campaign)

Organizing happens through building and sustaining relationships.

In some conversations, you end with an ask. Whether they agree and follow through on the ask tells us how ready they are to join the organizing effort. You might ask them to set up a meeting with another coworker, help create a list of coworkers' names, participate in an action, or sign a union card. It is critical to follow up with anyone you asked to do something. If you don't, you risk making the task seem unimportant. (Signing cards should happen on the spot to avoid this getting put off. If they can't do it right then, schedule a date and time to follow up.)

Organizing happens through building and sustaining relationships. You do that in one-on-ones and in social gatherings. The important thing is to get to know your coworkers, build trust, and learn about their issues. Then, it is important to help them feel the unfairness of their issues and the depth of their connection to fellow workers through those issues, as well as showing them how uniting allows us to overcome fear and build the power necessary to solve issues, and the importance of developing and carrying out organizing plans related to those issues.

Spotlight:
How Do You Organize in a Remote Workplace?

Organizing in remote workplaces is based on the same principles of in-person organizing. There are even perks: no boss walking by your desk, no anti-union coworker listening in. And you can talk to more people during the day on calls than you can at an office.

But it can be daunting to reach out to people you've never interacted with or met in person. Start with people you know and build your group from there! Find out who they know, what other teams you can connect with organically. Starting a conversation around a particular issue with a group of coworkers can be a tool to draw in new people.

" Vicky, software engineer, New York Times:

"I joined a lot of clubs when we first started organizing."

Don't worry about reaching out to someone you don't know – it's not as awkward as you think it might be. For the person on the other end of the line, having someone reach out to you to find out who you are, what you're up to, and how you're doing when you're mostly isolated can be nice. You can simply ask if they have time for a chat about some work stuff you'd like to get their thoughts on.

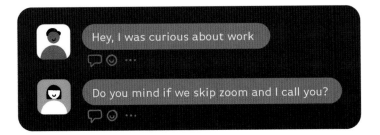

Move your conversations off company channels as soon as possible. And try to remember people's communication preferences: Do they like email or text? What apps do they already have on their phones?

🎙 JJ, gaming worker:

"A Signal group just sprung up with most of the workers at the company when we found out we were being acquired. You could see in that group who was agitated about certain issues and who might be easy to move."

Move your conversations off company channels as soon as possible.

Make it fun: If you're phone banking, set up a Zoom meeting with other members of your OC and make your calls while you're all together on Zoom. Create social and fun spaces for coworkers, bringing people together in person for social activities and organizing meetings. Or, make online meetings as engaging as you can. Sprinkle in fun social activities like online games or television viewing.

🎙 JJ, gaming worker:

"Our work Slack is a place where people come in at first very enthusiastically with their own hobbies and ideas. But it's quiet there, so it can feel alienating. But in our Discord, we can be lively. And through the Discord we started scheduling a lot of one-on-ones."

Consider opening a meme channel on Slack. Or, create a thread of "vibe checkers" for people to vote on how their day is going using emojis or GIFs, and message each other throughout the day about how they're doing. Plan online "coffee breaks" during work. Invite coworkers to a holiday party with online gift-giving or a Secret Santa.

" Hesh, Twitter tech worker:

"In the remote work context, people are alienated, and they crave connection with their coworkers. When you're in the office, it might be a pretty hard ask to ask someone to grab a coffee. It's going to cut into their day. But when we're remote, I can message people and say, 'I'm about to cook lunch, are you? Can we chat while we do that?' You can make it feel more informal and add less stress to their workday."

Collective action is also possible online! You might want to create a salary spreadsheet, where everyone shares what they are paid, or coordinate the answers to a company survey. You can change avatars or backgrounds to show support for the union, or collect workers' signatures and photos for a petition. You can plan slow-downs, work-to-rules, sick-outs, or even strike! (For definitions of these actions, see Lesson 3: Taking Collective Action and Escalating.)

Safety First!

Don't have an organizing Slack group on your work computer, or open your organizing chart on your work computer. Make sure everyone in your Slack group or Zoom call identifies who they are.

Lesson Three

Taking Collective Action And Escalating

Your campaign should be based on the issues, target decision-makers, and consist of a series of escalating actions, each of which after completing you should assess and build upon.

Your campaign's demands should be:

→ Definable, concrete, practical solutions with measurable outcomes
→ Based on widely and deeply felt issues
→ Relevant and life-changing
→ Compel people to organize

When identifying issues around which to organize, focus primarily on those that come up repeatedly in conversations with many coworkers across different jobs, and that have practical and measurable solutions.

Once you've identified the issues, you and your coworkers can develop a list of solutions. Those will be your demands around which you'll build an escalating campaign. After all, union drives are also based on changes people want to see.

Your biggest goals can only be won with the support of a majority of coworkers. But it's also true that taking action and winning demands helps build confidence and generates support from coworkers who may at first be reluctant to take action or sign a card.

The campaign must target people who have decision-making power — people who can change things. Identifying those people is a process called "power mapping." You will then also assess who are secondary targets — people that influence the decision-makers.

Your actions should:

→ Be focused on the issues
→ Move the campaign forward
→ Cause difficulties for your primary targets
→ Be something your coworkers feel ready and willing to do

The actions and messages you and your workers design should be well thought out and demonstrate the power of collective action, build solidarity, and test your strength. After each action, you'll assess as a group and decide on next steps.

Escalating "structure tests," such as coordinating to wear the same T-shirt on a given day and noting how many people participated in the action, can measure your level of support and also enable you to identify the departments/shifts where you have few supporters. You'll need to target those workers with one-on-ones and make other plans to move them. That way, when you need to take bold action, such as a strike, you know you are ready.

" Lucy, non-profit worker:

"When we first started organizing, it was about low wages for new workers. And when management responded to our pressure and increased pay, other workers who hadn't had courage before to sign on, signed on. They felt that that was only won because of our efforts. And now we're working for bereavement pay, COLA [cost-of-living adjustment], and time and a half for holidays.

"We started by asking for changes through approved channels. After management ignored our requests, we asked for a group meeting, which was also ignored. When we put forward proposals that management refused to engage with, it helped people realize that unionizing was important. Then we launched a social media campaign and held a rogue public event at the organization's farmers' market, where we were visible to consumers and donors. We set up a booth in the middle of the market even though we hadn't paid for the spot, demonstrating that we weren't afraid to ask for public support. We asked supporters who came to our table to sign postcards that we mailed into our workplace and posted those up on the bulletin boards and in the break room. Some of those supporters were donors."

📖 A **structure test** is an action by all or a majority of coworkers that demonstrates support for a demand or for unionization.

Below are some examples of actions you might take with your coworkers. Every workplace is different, and every group of coworkers is different, too. If you are exploring a big action in your workplace, you need to make sure you have the support to execute it. And be creative!

 Petition:
create a petition around a demand for your coworkers to sign.

2 March on the boss:
surprise the boss with a team meeting. Typically, in this action, workers take turns reading a prepared statement.

3 Sticker or button day:
all coworkers wear the same button or sticker on a given day.

4 Shirt day:
everyone wears the same color shirt or a pro-union shirt.

5 Work-to-rule:
when you and your coworkers strategically follow the company's stated rules and policies that, for efficiency's sake, are meant to be broken. This lowers your productivity and effectively creates a slow-down, but is practically non-disciplinable.

 Group breaks:
take a break with your coworkers.

 Slow-down:
everyone works slower.

8 Sick-out:
everyone calls out sick together.

9 Walk-out:
everyone leaves the job together for a period of time.

10 Strike:
everyone withholds their labor in response to the boss's union-busting tactics or bad-faith negotiating.

 Picket line:
this action often accompanying a strike will take place outside the workplace and discourage consumers and other workers from entering company property and allowing business to continue as normal. Crossing a picket line is considered a violation of the strike, and workers who engage in such behavior are often dubbed "scabs."

 Open-ended strike:
everyone withholds their labor for an indefinite amount of time.

When Should You Go Public?

Ideally, every secret campaign will eventually reveal itself through some kind of public action. To maximize your chances to win, public actions should involve clear roles and responsibilities, contingency plans, and logistical details. Successful public action will show your boss that you are organized, strong, and determined to win.

However, it's important to remember that engaging with the boss is a scary prospect for the vast majority of workers. You will need to prepare yourselves and your coworkers for the anxiety of confronting someone with direct power over you. Make sure to debrief with everyone who has had to directly confront the boss during an action, and help them process the experience so they come out feeling powerful.

In a union drive, the OC can take the campaign public once the following criteria are met:

→ The OC has connected to a supermajority of workers.

→ The OC has charted the workplace and its relationships.

→ The OC has a clear message and an understanding of the key issues.

→ The OC has conducted soft assessments of the workforce.

→ The OC believes it has enough support to withstand a strong anti-union campaign.

Generally, the campaign goes public by collecting signatures for a union election on authorization cards or a petition. Sometimes workers will march on the boss to demand voluntary union recognition.

We typically recommend that workers go public only once they have a full OC. Sometimes, if only a partial OC exists, the committee can seem more like a clique than a real leadership group. It takes time, honest assessments, and accountability to make sure the committee is composed of members who are respected by and representative of their peers.

After going public, the committee will need to keep in close contact with everyone to answer questions, counter the misinformation, help overcome fear and intimidation from the boss's anti-union campaign, and try to neutralize or win over the anti-union workers. The campaign message and actions should be geared toward the weak union supporters and the undecideds — not the workers who are strongly anti-union or strongly pro-union.

Can You Take Action Without a Majority?

When workers are stirred up about a shared issue and you can't wait for the slow work of building an OC or calling for an election, short but impactful collective actions against the managers may be called for.

Even without majority support, you can discuss what grievances you share with your coworkers, and act when you have a group that is ready. For medium-sized workplaces, which often have serious issues in one department that aren't shared across the whole workplace, actions taken by a minority of workers might also be useful. Worker groups can learn how to put pressure on the boss, articulate specific demands, and grow comfortable with explaining that the boss needs their cooperation to get the work done.

These tactics are especially useful when workers are stirred up about a shared concern that can be fixed relatively easily. Take these scenarios, for example:

→ Serious heat stress conditions, resolved with regular ten-minute cooling breaks

→ Unfair and serious discipline, replaced by progressive discipline

→ The elimination of late notice of mandatory overtime

Sometimes minority actions will accomplish small gains, which serve to encourage workers "on the fence" to believe that change is possible.

Inoculation & the Boss Campaign

Once you've decided you're ready to go public, it's very likely that your boss will push back. To win, you need to be prepared.

" James, Starbucks barista:

"We went public on Monday, and that same day, headquarters were on the phone with all the managers giving them guidance on what to do. One manager testified in an affidavit that they'd asked him to dig up dirt on people who'd been at the store for a very long time. He was forced to put out new schedules to make it more difficult for union supporters to talk to one another, and to staff the store with corporate store managers at every hour of the day.

"I wasn't so certain that the company, because of their progressive image, would respond so aggressively. But everything that happened at our store is exactly what was predicted by the people who were coaching us and giving us advice on how to prepare."

It's crucial to prepare your coworkers ahead of time for what management will do. This process of "inoculation" undercuts the power of the bosses' threats and messaging when they carry out those threats — and your coworkers will have more confidence in you and the union when they see that your predictions have come true.

Most anti-union campaigns follow a similar set of tactics. A highly paid union-buster will train management in anti-union arguments such as:

→ "The union is a third party, we won't be able to talk directly. We're a family!"

→ "Give us another chance, we're listening."

→ "Make sure to be informed, listen to both sides, and make your own decisions."

→ "The union can't guarantee you anything, you won't necessarily get the benefits you want or higher wages."

→ "The union just wants your dues money."

📕 **Third-Partying** is a term to describe union-busting rhetoric which asserts that the union is a separate entity from workers themselves. The intent is to undermine the collective and democratic nature of unions by creating the illusion of a third party that the workers are paying to speak on their behalf.

The Bosses' Tactics

The One-On-One

The boss will spread their anti-union arguments in one-on-one discussions so a worker will hear them in isolation. Managers may pull workers off the shop floor unannounced or will schedule job reviews. If you see management approaching workers in this manner, come up with a plan ahead of time for who will check in with the workers after they've been spoken to so they don't feel alone. Ideally, more than one person handles these check-ins.

If they identify vehemently anti-union workers, management will often lean on these individuals to spearhead their campaign, including by encouraging them to spread rumors about and create tensions with pro-union workers. Avoid direct confrontations with anti-union workers, and instead focus on workers with the weakest pro-union sentiments to ensure they aren't swayed by anti-union arguments.

A boss campaign deliberately creates a sense of discomfort and stress at work so that workers associate the union with that discomfort and stress.

The Captive Audience Meeting

Management will often hold captive meetings, which are mandatory sessions with groups of workers designed to communicate the company's opposition to unionization. In these meetings managers lay out a prepared anti-union script.

" Jordan, Trader Joe's worker:

"Our captive audience meetings were disguised as meetings called 'the huddle,' where a group of workers are gathered together with a manager and told about the very bad things that would happen if there was a union. This would include calling the union a 'third party,' emotional appeals, and straight-up lies like 'your schedule is going to change,' or 'your pay is going to be affected,' or 'you won't be able to talk to managers anymore.'

"There were also constant one-on-one conversations where coworkers would be specifically targeted: people who were shyer, seemingly susceptible to manipulation by the company, or people who were waiting for some kind of promotion. And any information we posted on the public bulletin board was taken down immediately, so it was really hard for us to get out information.

"The most effective thing they did was finding anti-union workers to do the work for managers and for the union-busting law firm. You can't file the same kind of charges against your coworkers as you would managers, and also, when your coworker is telling you something, it's a lot more emotional and effective than hearing it from a boss."

Don't let the boss control the narrative. Union supporters can interrupt and challenge the boss during these meetings, turning the boss's captive audience meeting into a workers' captive audience meeting.

Disciplining Organizers

Management may even go all out, disciplining workers, firing activists, or threatening to close the shop. Document everything! Document illegal threats, promises, discriminatory actions – but don't get sidetracked from organizing around your issues.

If you feel that you or one of your coworkers has been subjected to illegal disciplining for organizing, reach out to an EWOC organizer for support: workerorganizing.org/support.

An **Unfair Labor Practice** is an act that violates labor law. An employer often commits ULPs to undermine union activity. These should be reported to the NLRB, though the agency is often slow to resolve them. Filing ULPs cannot replace your organizing, but they can be grounds for going on strike.

Employer ULPs include: conducting any act of surveillance on organizing activities, or even the impression of such surveillance; offering promises if employees reject the union; forbidding workers from discussing work conditions or engaging in collective action; threatening with discipline for organizing, or implying that unionizing will not improve the workplace or have negative consequences; and any disciplinary action in retaliation for concerted activity.

Who Do You Inoculate and When?

Union-busting is primarily aimed at undecided workers, but you must prepare everyone for the boss campaign.

Consider any vulnerability a worker may have: a sick family member, attendance issues, or a strong desire for advancement – in case the boss uses that vulnerability against the individual. If workers know what's coming, they will recognize it for what it is. Don't let the bosses divide workers by language, race, department. They will try. Stress equality, justice, fairness.

Be sensitive to people's fears and don't pile on too much before they're ready. Instead, weave your inoculation into confidence-boosting discussions and activities. Throughout this ordeal, to win, you have to

The Union Busting Bingo Card

Make copies and use the Bingo card for fun and inspiration! Practice responding to the arguments in it with your coworkers. (You can even bring the cards when meeting with your boss to mark all the arguments they make!)

"The union is a 3rd party"	"Cards are legally binding"	"Restricted job titles and duties"	"Pizza party!"	"You will have to strike"
"Here's a quick fix!"	"Dues are expensive"	"We're already making those changes"	"If you don't like it then don't work here"	"People are unsigning"
"The union doesn't represent you"	"This could take years"	**Union busting is disgusting!** **Watch out for these tactics**	"This will affect your 401k"	"Give us a chance to fix things"
"The company is already listening"	"We already have affinity groups"	"This could hurt your career"	"No raises during negotiations"	"You can always come to us"
"You're making people uncomfortable"	"Organizing leads will get scheduled less"	"Here's a small raise!"	"We gave you parental leave"	"We're all making sacrifices"

keep talking about the issues that matter to workers and the organizing goals workers have set: wage increases, fair work schedules, fair treatment, democracy in the workplace. The union is the workers, and that is what the boss wants you to forget.

If workers know what's coming, they will recognize it for what it is.

" Jordan, Trader Joe's worker:

"We held a lot of meetings outside of work with coworkers to prepare them for what exactly to expect and followed up with people as they were confronted during the union-busting campaign. And we actually also had an inoculation party where we went over a bunch of things that people would hear from union-busting managers, and we worked out responses. We made a game night out of it."

Plan activities throughout to keep workers involved — rallies, cookouts, buttons, T-shirts, "We're Voting Yes" petitions. You use solidarity to combat fear, division, confusion, and hopelessness. By emphasizing transparency and democracy, workers can effectively disarm the argument that the union is something outside or above the workers.

Expose company lies with confidence. If your campaign is full of hope and solidarity, it will help workers overcome the fear that the union-buster spreads. United we win!

Spotlight:
The Multiracial, Multilingual Campaign

Labor organizing is based in solidarity, and racism undermines solidarity. Unfortunately, workplaces, like the rest of American society, are affected by racism. But whether from management or from coworkers, racial divisions serve the interests of the boss and weaken your collective power. Bosses know this and use every tool they can to sow division.

So, it's important to identify racism and fight it. Analyze structural racism in your workplace: Who gets hired? Who doesn't? What jobs are they hired into? Who gets promoted? Are there wage gaps within simi-

Your OC from the start should reflect the diversity of the workplace.

lar jobs? Are bosses — overtly or subtly — racist?

Look at instances of division such as: a restaurant whose personnel consists of white waitstaff and Latin American kitchen workers who make less and don't share the language or culture with the waitstaff; a warehouse where Black workers are assigned the heaviest, most dangerous jobs; a lunchroom where workers self-segregate.

From the start, your OC should reflect the diversity of the workplace. Find and recruit leaders from every ethnic group. If they are reluctant to get involved, you need to find out why. Fear? Prejudice? Privileges? Cultural differences? Language barriers? Immigration status? Leaders can explain how unifying benefits everyone.

Your OC should discuss which issues could unite workers across divisions, and address issues that arise in specific groups. Building a campaign around universal and specific grievances creates a stronger basis for solidarity and lasting unity. If language is a barrier, it might be necessary to create literature in multiple languages or find someone to serve as interpreter.

A good way to develop trusting relationships and shared understanding is by organizing social get-togethers such as picnics, cookouts, and sporting events. Choose an event location that will encourage the most reluctant group to come.

The OC can't avoid the subject of racism. You must talk about it, even at the risk of misspeaking. Organizers should listen to their coworkers and be willing to admit mistakes. The campaign must take principled stands against workplace racism, even if some coworkers object.

Unions can be a powerful institutional check on interpersonal racism, and fight to remove double standards in discipline policy and job classifications. Ultimately, fighting for fairness on the job will unite a majority.

When workers organize across ethnic and racial lines, everyone benefits. Wages of unionized workers are higher than those of non-union workers, and Black union workers earn higher wages than their non-union peers irrespective of race. When workers organize, they find they have a lot in common with each other — and that is what bosses fear.

Every Worker
Every-where

There is no single formula for organizing. Every campaign will be workplace-specific: the conditions will be unique; there will be different strengths and weaknesses on the part of both bosses and coworkers; goals may vary, and so may the most impactful organizing tactics.

That's why we encourage you to spend so much time meeting, talking, assessing, and reflecting with your coworkers on the work you're doing. We encourage you to seek support from experienced organizers. But you and your coworkers are the only true experts about your workplace, and know best what strategy will work for you.

One thing is always true: at its core, organizing is based on developing relationships with our coworkers and building a community where everyone is welcome. It's easy to organize your friends and people who already agree with you, but the key is to include people who aren't as easy to reach and find common cause with them.

It's hard, even overwhelming, to imagine being in solidarity with people in your workplace that don't share your worldview. But, in this polarized world, the workplace is actually one of the best places to foster solidarity, because workers are connected through their shared interests. Fighting for common demands to protect our livelihoods, families, and communities creates a powerful bond, one that can build a bigger and better movement.

The key to achieving a healthy society — where we enjoy both dignity on the job and living wages, where we have more time for rest and play, and where we can assert our rights freely without fear of retaliation — rests in our hands. It takes time and dedication because we're working within a world where democracy stops at the boss. But we have so much to win when we act together. We can accomplish almost anything.

Index

Further Reading

If you liked this book, you might also want to read...

Secrets of a Successful Organizer
Alexandra Bradbury, Mark Brenner and Jane Slaughter
labornotes.org

Them and Us Unionism
United Electrical, Radio and Machine Workers of America (UE)
ueunion.org

Class Struggle Unionism
Joe Burns

Rank and file Personal Histories
Alice and Staughton Lynd

The Long Deep Grudge: A Story of Big Capital, Radical Labor, and Class War in the American Heartland
Toni Gilpin

Labor's Untold Story
Richard O. Boyer and Herbert M. Morias

No Shortcuts: Organizing for Power
Jane McAlevey

On The Line
Daisy Pitkin

Solidarity Divided: The Crisis in Organized Labor and a New Path Toward Social Justice
Bill Fletcher Jr. and Fernando Gapasin

Acknowledgements

We have the deepest appreciation for the many EWOC volunteer organizers and supporters who contributed their knowledge, writing, and feedback to this guide, making it a product of the wisdom of the many. Many thanks to Eric Blanc, Alex Bradbury, Jenny Brown, Patrick Cate, Ian Cooper-Smith, Terry Davis, Marianela D'Aprile, Dan DiMaggio, Luis Feliz Leon, Prachi Goyal, Wes Holing, Roz Hunter, Bob Lawson, Ru Mehendale, Ian O'Hara, Shasta Payne, Colette Perold, Larson Ross, James Skretta, Dawn Tefft, Gabe Tobias, Micah Uetricht, Thurman Wenzl, and Grant West.

Special thanks to Megan Svoboda for shepherding the work of this organization since the beginning and supporting the development of this handbook.

Thanks also to the many others who've helped shape the content of our trainings, and by extension this guide, and to the workers who've organized their own workplaces and returned to share their stories and experiences with those who are newer to the movement.

We thank United Electrical, Radio and Machine Workers, Democratic Socialists of America, and Labor Notes for the continued support. We would not be the organization that we are if not for the long-standing labor left, the tradition in which we proudly stand. The knowledge we've shared here was retained by these organizations over the decades of their work.

Thanks also to our designer, Stephen Crowe, and the illustrators at Down the Street Designs, Paul Zappia and Remo Bangayan.

This was truly a labor of love and of dedication to workers organizing everywhere. Solidarity forever.